EUREKA!
I've discovered
S⊙UND

Suzanne Barchers

 Marshall Cavendish
Benchmark
New York

Marshall Cavendish Benchmark
99 White Plains Road
Tarrytown, NY 10591
www.marshallcavendish.us

All Internet addresses were available and accurate when this book went to press.

Library of Congress Cataloging-in-Publication Data
Barchers, Suzanne I.
I've discovered sound / by Suzanne I. Barchers.
p. cm. -- (Eureka!)
Includes bibliographical references and index.
ISBN 978-0-7614-3207-4
1. Sound--Juvenile literature. I. Title.
QC225.5.B348 2009
534--dc22
2008006477

Cover : Q2A Media Art Bank
Half Title: Vadim Ponomarenko/Shutterstock
Dennis Owusu-Ansah/ Shutterstock P7tr; Vadim Ponomarenko/Shutterstock P7br; Pinkcandy/
Dreamstime.com P7bl; leezsnow/istockphoto P7tl; leezsnow/istockphoto P7tl; Visual Arts Library
(London) / Alamy P11tl; Kmitu/Shutterstock P11bl; Imagestate RM/ Photolibrary : P12; Library of
Congress Prints and Photographs Division Washington P15tl; Stephen Leech/ Shutterstock P15tr;
jocicalek/ Shutterstock P15bl; iofoto/ Shutterstock P15br; Stephen Leech/ Shutterstock P15tr; Artem
Efimov/Shutterstock P19tr; Viktorus/ Dreamstime.com P19tl; James Steidl/ fotolia P19bl; Charles
Taylor/ Shutterstock P23tl; Danilo Ascione/ Shutterstock P23tr; Sjo/ istockphoto P23br; garysludden/
istockphoto P23bl; U.P.images_photo/ Shutterstock P23mr ; Dreamstime.com P27tl; kristian sekulic/
Shutterstock P27tr; Holger Mette/ Shutterstock P27bl; Emanon/ Dreamstime.com P27br
Illustrations: Q2A Media Art Bank

Created by Q2AMedia
Creative Director: Simmi Sikka
Series Editor: Jessica Cohn
Art Director: Sudakshina Basu
Designer: Dibakar Acharjee
Illustrators: Amit Tayal, Aadil Ahmed, Rishi Bhardwaj, Kusum Kala, Pooja Shukla and Sanyogita Lal
Photo research: Sejal Sehgal
Senior Project Manager: Ravneet Kaur
Project Manager: Shekhar Kapur

Printed in Malaysia

1 3 5 6 4 2

Contents

Now Hear This!   4

Listen Closely   8

Can You Hear Me?   12

That Machine Talks   16

Turn Up the Radio!   20

Ping . . . Ping . . . Ping   24

Timeline   28

Glossary   30

Index   32

Now Hear This!

Did you ever get water in your ears—and find that you couldn't hear much, or that your hearing was muffled? What a relief it was when you got the water out of your ears. You could hear sounds again.

Everything you hear starts with a **vibration**. Touch your throat and read this next sentence aloud: *I can feel the vibration in my throat.* Any sound—your own voice, the phone ringing, your favorite song, a dog barking—starts with vibrations.

Alfonso Corti was a scientist with an interest in medicine. If he could tell you how sound works . . .

Meet Alfonso Corti

Alfonso Corti (1822–1876) was the son of a rich Italian **marquis**. When his father died in 1851, Corti became the marquis and inherited his wealth. Until then, Corti worked on medical research. In 1847, he went to medical school in Vienna, Austria. As part of his training, he learned how a reptile's bloodstream works. Then he studied the ears of mammals. In 1851, he discovered a **membrane** attached to the **cochlea** deep inside the **inner ear**. He learned that thousands of tiny hairs are attached to this membrane. When the membrane vibrates, those tiny hairs turn the vibrations into a message that is sent to the brain. This message is similar to the computer message, "You've got mail!" It gets the brain's attention. This tiny but important part of the ear is called the **organ of Corti**.

AAHHHHHHH

A balloon pops.

The sound waves travel to the **outer ear**.

The sound waves travel through the ear canal to the **middle ear**.

The sound waves vibrate against the **ear-drum**.

The sound waves make three tiny bones vibrate. These bones are nicknamed **the hammer, anvil, and stirrup.**

The vibrations travel to the inner ear and to the cochlea.

Tiny **hair cells** inside the cochlear nerve tell the brain that a **balloon popped.**

Make a Model of the Ear

You Will Need:

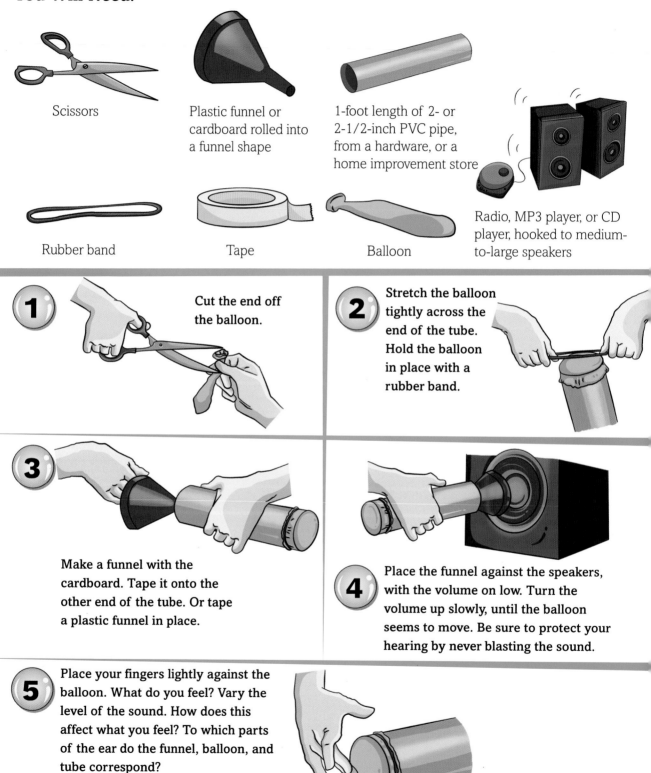

Scissors

Plastic funnel or cardboard rolled into a funnel shape

1-foot length of 2- or 2-1/2-inch PVC pipe, from a hardware, or a home improvement store

Radio, MP3 player, or CD player, hooked to medium-to-large speakers

Rubber band

Tape

Balloon

1 Cut the end off the balloon.

2 Stretch the balloon tightly across the end of the tube. Hold the balloon in place with a rubber band.

3 Make a funnel with the cardboard. Tape it onto the other end of the tube. Or tape a plastic funnel in place.

4 Place the funnel against the speakers, with the volume on low. Turn the volume up slowly, until the balloon seems to move. Be sure to protect your hearing by never blasting the sound.

5 Place your fingers lightly against the balloon. What do you feel? Vary the level of the sound. How does this affect what you feel? To which parts of the ear do the funnel, balloon, and tube correspond?

WHO WOULD HAVE THOUGHT?

Those tiny hairs inside the organ of Corti make it possible for you to hear. You have about 15,000 hair cells in each ear. That seems like a lot, but once they are damaged, they can't be fixed. Loud noises—even your favorite music—can damage those hairs and cause hearing loss. That's why you'll see lots of workers—especially musicians—wearing **ear protectors**.

Listen Closely

In the 1800s, doctors had only one way to listen to the lungs or heart. They would rest an ear against the patient's chest and listen. René Laënnec was a young doctor in Paris in 1816. He needed to listen to a woman patient's heart and lungs, but Laënnac had two problems. First of all, he was a bit embarrassed to place his ear against her chest. The second problem was that she was plump. That would make it difficult for him to hear her heart and lungs in the usual way. Suddenly Laënnec had a brainstorm.

He knew that you could put your ear on a beam of wood and hear a pin being scratched at the other end. The doctor wondered if sound would travel the same way from inside the chest. He then rolled up a stack of paper and made a funnel of sorts. He put the small end to his ear and the big end on her chest. It worked!

This works for the lungs, too.

Meet René Laënnec

René Laënnec (1781–1826) spent a few years improving his idea. He found that a hollow tube of wood worked well. He named his invention the **stethoscope**, from the Greek words for "chest" and "to see." He and other doctors used the stethoscope to treat **tuberculosis**, a deadly disease of the lungs. The stethoscope made it possible for doctors to hear the lungs clearly. When Laënnec was forty-five years old he got very sick. His own invention confirmed that he had tuberculosis.

Make Your Own Stethoscope

You Will Need:

Large plastic funnel

15 to 20 inches of 1/2-inch flexible tubing

Household items that make noise, such as a ticking clock

Note: Tubing is found in hardware or automotive stores. In fact, a transmission oil funnel, found in automotive departments, comes with tubing attached, for just a couple of dollars.

1 Stretch one end of the tubing over the narrow part of a funnel.

2 Find things in your house to listen to: a running dishwasher, a ticking clock, a timer that buzzes or rings, an iPod, the television, your refrigerator, etc.

3 Listen carefully to the first object with an ear against it.

4 Place the funnel on the object. Place the tube carefully by your ear. How is the sound changed?

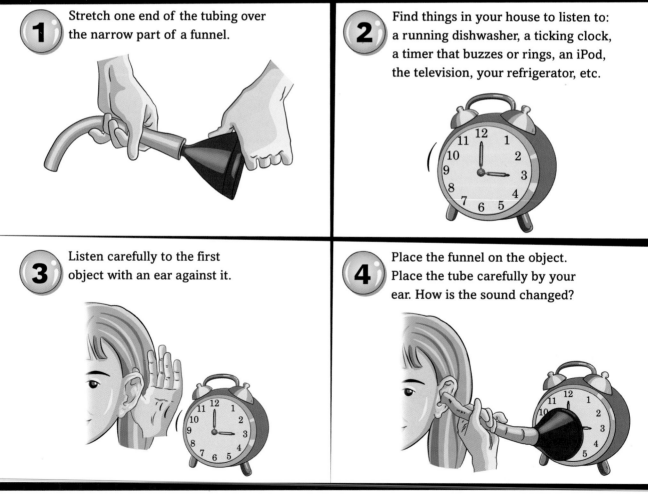

WHO WOULD HAVE THOUGHT?

Though many people first thought the stethoscope was unnecessary, René Laënnec's invention was adopted by doctors. Thirty years later, his one-ear stethoscope was replaced with a model that could be used with both ears. A stethoscope with two tubes and two earpieces, like the kind used today, was invented in 1855. Next time you have a check-up, see if your doctor knows who invented the first stethoscope.

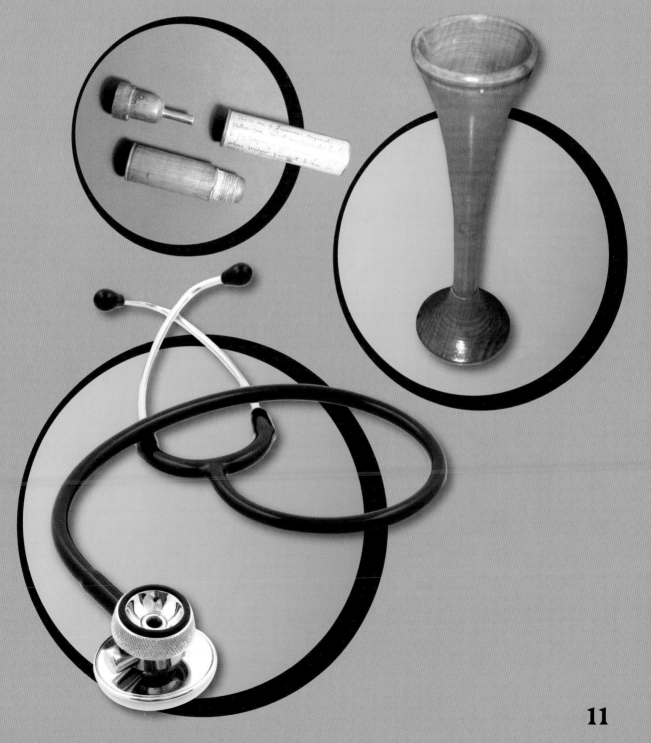

Can You Hear Me?

Inventors do not always set out to invent things. Thomas Watson's first job was bookkeeping, but he found it boring. Alexander Graham Bell (1847–1922) began his career by helping deaf people learn to speak, just as his father and grandfather had done. His experience with deaf people led Bell to think about how sound travels. From there, he went on to invent the **telephone**. He got Thomas Watson, who was working in a machine shop by then, to help him. The two began to experiment with the **telegraph**—which sent messages in a code based on clicking sounds. They figured out that a machine that sent clicks could be fixed to send other sounds. Like most inventions, their project progressed through trial and error. They played with **electromagnets** and **receivers** until they got the right result.

Finally! The human voice can truly travel!

Meet Thomas Watson

Thomas Watson (1854–1934) brought skills he learned in the machine shop to Bell's lab. The day their telephone finally worked, they were working in different rooms. Bell spilled acid on his arm. Talking into their new machine, he exclaimed, "Mr. Watson, come here. I want you." Watson heard Bell clearly. That was the moment they knew the telephone was ready. Given the accident, it was good timing for a voice to travel!

It was good timing in more ways than one. Several inventors were working on voice machines at the same time. In 1876, Bell went to the **U.S. Patent Office** to claim rights to the telephone. Just hours after Bell made his claim, an inventor named Elisha Gray showed up to do the same thing. Watson was a young man when Bell and he invented the telephone. In just a few years he became wealthy as a result of their invention.

Experiment with Sound

You Will Need:

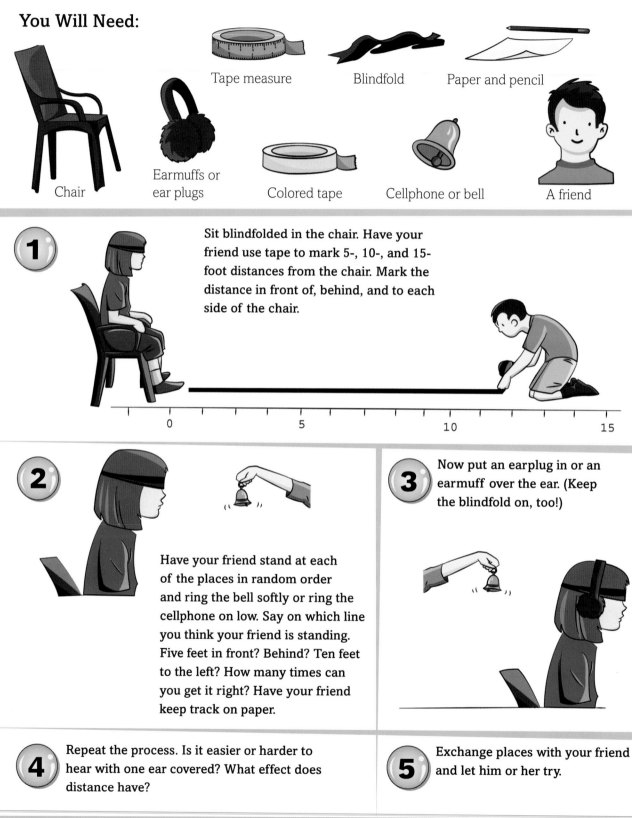

Tape measure

Blindfold

Paper and pencil

Earmuffs or ear plugs

Chair

Colored tape

Cellphone or bell

A friend

1 Sit blindfolded in the chair. Have your friend use tape to mark 5-, 10-, and 15-foot distances from the chair. Mark the distance in front of, behind, and to each side of the chair.

0   5   10   15

2 Have your friend stand at each of the places in random order and ring the bell softly or ring the cellphone on low. Say on which line you think your friend is standing. Five feet in front? Behind? Ten feet to the left? How many times can you get it right? Have your friend keep track on paper.

3 Now put an earplug in or an earmuff over the ear. (Keep the blindfold on, too!)

4 Repeat the process. Is it easier or harder to hear with one ear covered? What effect does distance have?

5 Exchange places with your friend and let him or her try.

WHO WOULD HAVE THOUGHT?

From 1876 to now, phones have changed. Phones have become smaller and smaller. Wires aren't needed to connect phones any more. **Cellphones** use **satellites** in outer space to send signals. People can even send text messages by phone. What would Bell and Watson think if they saw you talking on a cellphone as small as your hand?

THIS MODEL OF BELL'S FIRST
TELEPHONE IS A DUPLICATE OF THE INSTRU'
MENT THROUGH WHICH SPEECH SOUNDS WERE
FIRST TRANSMITTED ELECTRICALLY, 1875.

That Machine Talks

Some of the greatest inventions happen almost by accident. By 1877, Thomas A. Edison had been inventing machines and new materials for several years. He had already made improvements to the telephone. He had figured out how to record a telegraph's dots and dashes on a long strip of paper. This paper could be used to send messages without an operator. All that work led up to one his most famous inventions.

Imagine if he could tell you the story today:

Meet Thomas Alva Edison

Thomas Alva Edison (1847–1931) was another inventor who was interested in how sound works. In his case it was because he had lost most of his hearing when he was twelve years old. Even as a teenager, he loved to experiment with ideas and machines. As an adult, he raced other inventors, such as Alexander Graham Bell, to make the best machines for sending voices over distances. Edison is probably most famous for making an electric light bulb that could glow for over 1,500 hours. He was not the first to make an electric light, but he made major improvements to the design. Edison loved inventing so much, he built an "invention factory" in Menlo Park, New Jersey.

I'LL RACE YOU!

I was playing around with a **stylus**—and I noticed that moving it across **grooves** on **paraffin paper** made noises.

I knew I was onto something, so I took apart a telephone. I thought maybe the vibrations of the speaker could make marks on the paper.

The paper didn't work well. So I kept experimenting with different things. Finally, I tried putting **tinfoil** on a **cylinder**. I put the stylus on the tinfoil, turned the cylinder with a crank, and started talking.

I said, "Hello! Mary had a little lamb."

It worked. I could hear myself!

Make a Sound Machine

You Will Need:

Sheet of plastic wrap

Rubber band

Variety of loud noisemakers: for example, a whistle, a metal pan and spoon, a bell

Large round bowl or pan

1 tablespoon uncooked rice, salt, or cereal

1 Stretch the plastic wrap over the bowl or pan. If you don't have the stretchy kind, use a rubber band to hold it down.

2 Work in an area that can be easily swept. Scatter the rice, salt, or cereal on the top of the plastic wrap.

3 Make a noise nearby. What happens to the material that's on top of the wrap?

4 Experiment by moving the noisemaker closer or farther away. Try putting the items on different surfaces (wooden table, glass table, kitchen chair). Does anything change?

WHO WOULD HAVE THOUGHT?

Long before MP3 players, people listened to music on **phonographs**. It took a while for the phonograph to catch on, but not because people didn't like music. In 1899, a phonograph cost $125. That's almost $3,000 in today's dollars! You also needed special cylinders to hear some of the music. Each cylinder cost $4—more than $80 in today's money. Since then, music players have become smaller and less expensive. Now, you can carry recorded music in your pocket.

Turn Up the Radio!

In the late 1800s, inventors were tinkering with the idea of sending messages without wires. Guglielmo Marconi became famous for his work on the telegraph. He figured out how to send messages with **electromagnetic** or **"radio" waves**. Those messages were hard to understand, however. It took Reginald Fessenden to make the idea work. He became known as the "Father of Radio."

If he could tell his story, it might sound like this:

Meet Reginald Fessenden

Reginald Fessenden's (1866–1932) parents wanted him to become a teacher or a minister, but he had other ideas. He went to work for Thomas Edison. Fessenden learned about electricity. In time, he invented a radio that could work over long distances. December 24, 1906, was a historic day for him and for the world. He hosted the first live **radio broadcast** of music and readings from the Bible.

A telegraph operator on the S.S. *Kroonland* was listening for messages while traveling across the Atlantic Ocean. Suddenly, instead of hearing telegraphed clicks, he heard a woman singing. It seemed like a miracle.

MY NEXT INVENTION SHOULD BE HOW TO SWITCH STATIONS!

I knew there had to be a better way of sending radio waves. The sound waves needed to be continuous.

I used what I knew about electricity to build a **transmitter** that sent out waves continuously and a lot faster. So I built a **generator**.

I was experimenting with my generator in December of 1900. My assistant was about 50 miles away. I hooked up a **microphone** to the generator and started talking to my assistant.

"One, two, three, four. Is it snowing where you are, Mr. Thiessen? If so, telegraph back and let me know."

He telegraphed back that it was snowing! And that was just the beginning.

Receiving Radio Signals

You Will Need:

Your ear

Source of music,
such as a radio

Your hands

10 or so pieces of paper,
rolled up and taped into
the shape of a cone

Small kitchen funnel

1 Roll your paper into the shape of a cone, with a small open end on one side and a larger open end on the other. Roll your cone so that the larger open end is wider than the larger opening on the funnel.

2 Turn on the radio or other source of music at low volume. First try listening with your ears alone. Point one ear toward the sound source.

3 Then cup your hand over the ear pointed to the sound source. See if that helps you to hear better. Remove your hand and listen again without the aid of your cupped hand.

4 Repeat with the funnel. Hold the small end of the funnel next to your ear, with the larger end toward the sound. Caution: Do not push the funnel into the ear canal.

5 Repeat with the rolled-up paper.

6 The ears alone have the smallest area for sound waves to enter. The cupped hand is wider than the ear hole alone. The funnel is larger still. The cone is even larger. How might this sound wave experiment be applied to the way that radio signal receivers are shaped?

WHO WOULD HAVE THOUGHT?

Reginald Fessenden's work resulted in more than five hundred patents. Several of his inventions were used during World War II. These include the radio pager, or **beeper**, and the **depth sounder**. They also include the **tracer bullet**, **radio compass**, and **voice scrambler**. Your parents might even use one of his inventions—an **automatic garage door opener**.

Ping . . . Ping . . . Ping

If you've seen the ocean, you know how huge, dark, and deep it can be. Not being able to see in deep water was a problem for Great Britain and the United States during World War I. The Germans had invented the submarine and were using it for attacks.

In 1915, a German submarine **torpedoed** the British ship *Lusitania*. The ship sank in less than twenty minutes. More than one thousand people died.

That is when Paul Langévin started work on a machine that could "see" beneath the sea. He wanted to help find and destroy the submarines.

Langévin figured out how to detect sounds as far away as 655 feet (200 meters). Yet that wasn't good enough to help much in the sea battles of World War I. So he started experimenting with sending out a high-frequency "chirp" and timing the echo.

That was the answer!

This device, called **SONAR**, for **SO**und **NA**vigation and **R**anging, was too late for World War I. When World War II started, however, the U.S. and British forces were ready for enemy submarines.

The **echo** tells me how far away the **submarine** might be.

Meet Paul Langévin

Born in France, Paul Langévin (1872–1946) was a gifted scientist who was active in social causes. He believed in human rights and peace—and spoke out against the Nazis. In 1940, he was arrested by the Germans. Fortunately, he escaped to Switzerland in 1944. Langévin was also fortunate to know other great scientists of his time. He knew Albert Einstein, who came up with famous theories about energy, and Marie Curie, the well-known chemist. In fact, Langévin's grandson married Marie Curie's granddaughter.

Experiment with SONAR

You Will Need:

Slinky®, sold at toy and party stores

3 handballs, or rubber balls 2-1/2-inches wide, and 3 assistants to bounce them

Chair

Short stepladder

1 First, show how sound waves travel by stretching a Slinky between yourself and a friend. Don't stretch it too far. Give a quick push to the Slinky. The "waves" move away like sound waves. With enough of a push, the waves bounce back, much like sound waves bounce back in SONAR. Practice a few times to see both effects.

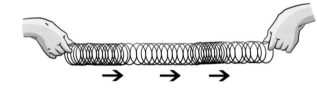

2 Next, ask an assistant to stand on the stepladder. Have one friend sit on the floor. Have the other sit on the chair.

3 Practice saying, "One-two-three-drop!" a few times. Each person needs to drop the rubber ball at the same time and then catch it when it bounces up. (No one should throw the ball down; just let it drop.)

4 Once you are ready, drop the balls on the count of three. Your assistants should say, "Caught!" when they catch their balls.

5 Ask: Which ball takes the longest to catch? How does that relate to SONAR? How could this be used to find the different depths of the ocean floor?

WHO WOULD HAVE THOUGHT?

Sound waves are important to animals, too. Whales, dolphins, seals, and porpoises send out "clicks" or sound pulses. They hope that the echoes will tell them where they can find their next meal. Bats use a kind of SONAR, too. Their sounds are so high-pitched that humans can't hear them. The bats use the echoes to navigate. So the next time someone uses the expression, "blind as a bat," you can explain about **echolocation** and that bats "see" just fine.

Timeline

HHHHHHHAA

1816
René Laënnec invents the first stethoscope.

1851
Alfonso Corti discovers the organ of Corti.

1876
Thomas Watson assists Alexander Graham Bell with the invention of the telephone.

1906
Reginald Fessenden
invents the radio.

1877
Thomas Alva Edison
invents the phonograph.

1916
Paul Langévin invents
what becomes known as
SONAR in 1918.

Glossary

beeper Device that can receive messages and alert the user to them.

cellphone Wireless telephone that sends and receives signals using satellites and signal towers.

cochlea Snail-shaped part of the inner ear that holds the organ of Corti.

cylinder Object that has a round base and straight sides.

depth sounder Device that measures how deep the water is under a ship.

ear-drum Thin membrane that separates the outer ear from the middle ear.

ear protectors Often referred to as earplugs, they help prevent hearing loss from noise.

echolocation Use of sound to locate objects by collecting echoes that bounce back from these objects.

electromagnet Metal core wrapped with wire coil that acts like a magnet when electric current flows through the wire.

electromagnetic Type of energy formed in waves, such as radio waves and light waves.

generator Machine that changes mechanical energy to electrical energy.

garage door opener, automatic Device that signals a motor to raise or lower a garage door.

grooves Tracks in a record for the **stylus** or needle to follow.

hair cells In the organ of Corti, the tiny receptors for what mammals hear.

inherited To have received something of value from people who lived before you.

inner ear Deepest part of the ear; contains the organ of Corti and the cochlea.

marquis Type of nobleman in some European countries.

membrane Thin layer of tissue.

microphone Device that changes sound into an electrical signal.

middle ear Part of the ear between the ear-drum and the inner ear.

organ of Corti Organ deep in the inner ear that has hair cells that send messages about what is being heard to the brain.

outer ear Part of the ear that can be seen.

paraffin paper Paper lightly coated with a waxy substance.

phonograph Device that plays recorded sound.

radio broadcast Spoken or musical program sent by radio waves.

radio compass Device that tracks the location of incoming radio waves.

radio waves Electromagnetic waves used to send information. See **electromagnetic**.

receiver The part of a radio that receives the incoming signals or waves.

satellite Device designed for communication that orbits in space.

SONAR (SOund NAvigation and Ranging) Technology that uses echoes to locate objects under water.

stethoscope Device for listening to the internal sounds of the body.

stylus Like a pen, used for writing or making marks on something other than paper.

telegraph System that sends and receives messages by sending electric impulses over wire.

telephone Instrument that changes sounds into signals for sending and receiving.

tinfoil Paper-thin sheet of metal; usually aluminum or a combination of tin and lead.

torpedo Explosive device fired from a submarine.

tracer bullet Bullet that marks its path with a trail of smoke or light.

transmitter Device that sends electromagnetic signal.

tuberculosis Disease that affects the lungs, causing coughing, fever, chest pain, and, sometimes, death.

U.S. Patent Office Government office that grants patents to inventors. A patent is an official document awarded by the government giving an inventor the exclusive right to make and sell something.

vibration Back and forth movement in a regular pattern.

voice scrambler Device that mixes up audio signals.

Index

anvil, 5
beeper, 23
Bell, Alexander Graham, 12, 13, 15, 17, 28
cellphone, 14, 15
cochlea, 5
Corti, Alfonso, 4, 5, 7, 28
Curie, Marie, 25
depth sounder, 23
ear canal, 5, 22
ear protector, 7
ear-drum, 5
echolocation, 27
Edison, Thomas A., 16, 17, 21, 29
Einstein, Albert, 25
electric light bulb, 17
electromagnet, 12, 20
Fessenden, Reginald, 20, 21, 23, 29
generator, 21
Gray, Elisha, 13
hair cell, 5, 7
hammer, 5
heart, 8
inner ear, 5
Laënnec, René, 8, 9, 11, 28
Langévin, Paul, 24, 25, 29
lung, 8, 9
Lusitania, 24
Marconi, Guglielmo, 20
marquis, 5
membrane, 5
Menlo Park, 17
microphone 21
middle ear, 5

music, 7, 19, 21, 22
nerve, 5
organ of Corti, 7, 28
outer ear, 5
outer space, 15
paraffin paper, 17
phonograph, 19, 29
radio, 6, 20, 21, 22, 23 29
receiver, 12, 22
S.S. Kroonland, 21
satellite, 15
scrambler, 23
SONAR, 24, 26, 27, 29
sound wave, 5, 21, 22, 26, 27
stethoscope, 9, 10, 11, 28
stirrup, 5
stylus, 17
telegraph, 12, 16, 20, 21
telephone, 12, 13, 16, 17, 28
torpedo, 24
transmitter, 21
tuberculosis, 9
U.S. Patent Office, 13
vibration, 4, 5, 17
voice, 4, 12, 13, 17, 23
Watson, Thomas, 12, 13, 15, 28
wire, 15, 20
World War I, 24
World War II, 23, 24